The Amana People

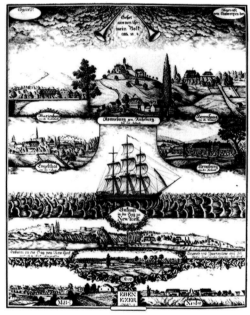

Joseph Prestele, Sr.

From Germany to America, 1844

Behold the work of the old.
Let your heritage not be lost,
but bequeath it as a memory,
treasure and blessing.
Gather the lost and the hidden,
and preserve it for your children.

—Christian Metz, 1846

The Amana People

The History of a Religious Community

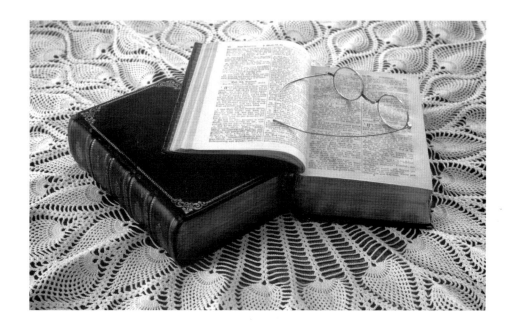

By Peter Hoehnle

About the Author

The author, Peter Hoehnle, is a Ph.D. candidate at Iowa State University and a life-long Amana resident.

Acknowledgments

In addition to those listed with contributed photographs, a special thank you to the Amana Heritage Society; Erma Kellenberger and Arthur Selzer for use of photographs; and Karen Jenkins, Lanny Haldy, Barbara Hoehnle, Dorothy Schweider, Emilie Hoppe, Janet Zuber, Marietta Moershel, Lina Unglenk, Mary Bennett, and Jonathan Andelson.

Editors: Joan Liffring-Zug and Dwayne M. Bourret, Maureen Patterson, Dorothy Crum, Julie Eisele, Melinda Bradnan, Miriam Canter, Stephanie Schatz, and Jordan Heusinkveld

Graphics: M. A. Cook Design, Molly Cook

Photographs: Joan Liffring-Zug Bourret
Front cover: Poppies in South Amana
Back cover: Henrietta Moershel's peonies, Homestead
Title page: Placed atop a handmade Amana tablecloth are copies of the Bible and the *Psalter-Spiel*, the Amana hymnal.

Other photographers are credited, if known, with their photographs. Bertha M.H. Shambaugh of Iowa City was the first outsider to extensively photograph Amana people and village scenes. Although official church doctrine labeled photography a worldly practice and suggested that it ran counter to the second commandment against making graven images, several Amana residents were active in photographing the community. Well over 6,000 images of communal Amana are part of the photographic archive of the Amana Heritage Society, suggesting that, at best, the elders were lax in enforcing the prohibition on photography. These photographers ordered much of their equipment through catalogues, and most of them processed their own glass plates and, later, flexible film negatives in basement corner dark rooms.

© 2003 Peter Hoehnle   ISBN 1-93204351-9   Library of Congress 2003104481

Contents

Dedication

To my two Amana *Omas,*
Helene Hergert Hoehnle (1907–2000)
and Marie Stuck Selzer (1916–1999)

 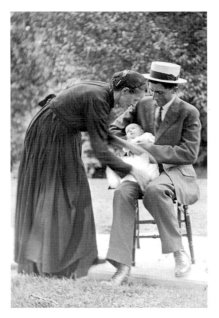

Left: *The author's great-grandfather, Middle Amana cobbler Carl Hergert, Sr. (1883–1972), is seen here with daughters Helene (left) and Marie on the steps of their home, circa 1915.*

Right: *In this 1916 photograph, Marie Stuck Selzer is in the lap of her father, Peter Stuck (1890–1979), with grandmother, Susanna Trautmann Moershel (1866–1938), standing.*

Three Hundred Years of Faith

The Amana Society was a religious communal society located in east central Iowa. Founded by the Community of True Inspiration, a Pietistic German religious sect that originated in 1714, the Society practiced communal living for almost ninety years, making it among the largest and longest lasting of America's communal groups. Following a decline in religious enthusiasm, a youth revolt, and the staggering effects of the Great Depression, Society members voted to reorganize their community as a stock corporation in 1932.

Today, the Amana Society Inc. continues to manage the surviving business interests of the old community, including Iowa's largest private farm, while the Amana Church Society keeps alive the spiritual traditions of the community. In recent years, the Amanas have become a popular destination for visitors from around the world.

The Amana Inspirationists are often confused with the Amish, with whom they share little beyond the use of the German language, emphasis on personal religious devotion, and simplicity in religious observances. The unfortunate similarity of the names of the two sects is the primary source of the confusion. Unlike the Amish, members of the Amana Society have always embraced technology and sent their children to public schools; they also do not practice shunning and are not Anabaptists. The people of the Amana Society were part of a larger trend toward communal living practiced by thousands of social reformers and religious groups during the nineteenth century. Although many of these organizations lasted less than a year, others, such as the Shakers, the Oneida Community of New York, the Society of Separatists at Zoar, Ohio, the Harmony Society of Pennsylvania, and the Hutterites flourished for generations.

The longest-lived of these groups, like the Amana Society, were more focused on developing a simple religious lifestyle than in promoting larger reforms in the world outside their communities.

While many communal societies vanished, leaving little to mark their existence, the Amana Society's successful reorganization into separate church and business organizations has ensured that the religious and economic legacy of the original Society will endure.

During its communal period, the Society printed a brief history that it distributed to curious visitors. That history is both long out of print and somewhat dated in its methodology and style. This book is a brief overview of the Amana community, from its founding in Germany to the present day. Several detailed books and articles have been written about Amana and are noted in the bibliography. Many of the illustrations in this work are printed here for the first time.

Be still and know that the Angel of the Lord,
who has protected you,
will be with you wherever you shall go.
Trust in the Lord, the King of Kings, your Jesus,
and let His sacred Spirit strengthen
the harmony and understanding within you;
then the peace of God will be with you always.

—Johann Friedrich Rock, 1736

The Community of True Inspiration

The Castle of Refuge

Watercolor painting of the Ronneburg Castle, circa 1830, unknown artist. For more than a century, the Ronneburg served as a refuge for the Community of True Inspiration, the sect that later founded the Amana Society.

Joan Liffring-Zug Bourret photograph, 1980s

South Amana meetinghouse, built in 1871. Grapes and flower gardens pictured belong to a nearby resident. Amana meetinghouses built of brick or sandstone were in the centers of the villages, an easy walk for the residents. Each meetinghouse had separate entrances for men and women, who sat on separate sides. The interiors were painted blue. During the communal period, eleven services were held weekly but only one in the meetinghouse. Additional evening prayer services were held in designated homes in the villages. Elders conducted all services.

The Community of True Inspiration

Nestled in the wooded valley of the Iowa River in east central Iowa, the seven villages of the Amana Colonies retain ample evidence of the work of the sturdy German Pietists who settled and constructed the villages a century and a half ago. Refugees from religious persecution, the founders of Amana were the descendants of an eighteenth-century religious movement first known as the Community of True Inspiration *(Wahre Inspirations Gemiende)*.

The origins of the Amana Society can be found in the Pietist Movement of the early eighteenth century. Dissatisfied with the dogmatism and formality of the established church, the Pietists, under such leaders as Auguste Francke, sought to invigorate religious experience and service through a return to simpler forms. For some Pietists this meant leaving most of the trappings of the established church, including the church hierarchy, a formal liturgy, regular sacraments, and ostentatious church ornamentation, and replacing them with simple gatherings featuring *a cappella* singing, unadorned worship places, and ecstatic, extemporaneous worship.

In the early 1700s, former Lutheran clergyman Eberhard Ludwig Gruber (1655–1728) and saddle maker Johann Friedrich Rock (1678–1749) began to meet and discuss scripture and Pietistic thought. Both had relocated to Himbach, located in the liberal region of the Wetterau, whose leaders promised protection to separatists, Jews, and other religious minorities, hoping they would repopulate the region devastated in the Thirty Years War. In 1714 a group of mystical Pietists known as the *Inspirirte,* or "the inspired," came to their attention.

Although he initially rejected the Inspired's claim that they possessed the gift of divine inspiration, Gruber invited representatives of the group to a meeting in his home on November 15, 1714, and he was converted. The next day, November 16, 1714, a small group, including Rock and Gruber, again gathered for worship. The Community of True Inspiration traces its foundation to this meeting, after which both Gruber and Rock became active supporters of the sect.

Gruber assumed leadership of the sect, while Rock became one of its *Werkzeuge*, or "inspired instruments." During the period 1714–1720, ten individuals, including three women, served as *Werkzeuge*. The *Werkzeuge* of this period were, in order of their first testimony:

Johann Tobias Pott (1691–1759)
Johann Heinrich Pott (1692–1777)
August Friedrich Pott (1695–1777)
Johanna Margaretha Melchior (1690–1751)
Eva Catharina Wagner (dates unknown)
Johann Adam Gruber (1693–1763)
Johann Friedrich Rock (1678–1749)
Johann Melchior Schwanfelder (dates unknown)
Ursula Mayer (dates unknown)
Johann Carl Gleim (dates unknown)

The *Werkzeuge* delivered testimonies while traveling across what is today Germany, Switzerland, and the present Czech Republic, accompanied by scribes who recorded their testimonies as they were spoken, to be published later. Most were inspired for short periods, ranging from three months to a few years. Testimonies were often preceded by a period of *Bewegungen,* during which the *Werkzeug* shook uncontrollably. Sometimes testimonies were delivered in written form and were known as *Einsprache*, in contrast to the spoken testimonies that were known as *Aussprache*. After 1720, Rock remained the group's only *Werkzeug* and, as such, made more than ninety-four journeys to Inspirationist congregations scattered across the German states.

Following E.L. Gruber's death on December 11, 1728, Rock assumed leadership of the sect and continued in this capacity until his death on March 2, 1749, after which his scribe Paul Nagel, trained as an attorney, became the group's leader and continued to visit the scattered congregations and minister to the faithful. During much of this period, the center of the Inspirationist movement remained the Ronneburg Castle, a massive thirteenth-century structure whose owner, Prince Ysenburg, leased to a diverse community of Moravians, Jews, Inspirationists, and religious separatists who sought his protection. Nagel continued to visit the far-flung Inspirationist congregations and maintain activity within the sect, despite the fact that it no longer possessed a *Werkzeug*. Following Nagel's death in 1779, however, the group entered a period of decline that did not end until 1817, when virtually all of its original leaders and mainstays had died. In that year Michael Krausert, a journeyman tailor from Strassburg, proclaimed that he was an inspired *Werkzeug* and made himself known to the Inspirationist communities.[1]

Krausert's emergence led to dissension within the dying movement because some leaders and congregations refused to accept him as a true *Werkzeug*. Krausert, however, gained followers and began to instigate a revival. In 1818, Barbara Heinemann (1795–1883), an illiterate serving maid from Alsace, was directed to the Inspirationists by friends who felt her strange visions and inner promptings were similar to those of an Inspirationist *Werkzeug*. Krausert accepted Heinemann at once, and she began to speak in Inspiration alongside her mentor.[2]

In 1819, Christian Metz (1794–1867), a carpenter who was born and reared within the Inspirationist community, also began to speak in Inspiration. When Metz was six, his family relocated to Ronneburg Castle, where he spent his formative years and learned carpentry. As a young man, Metz joined with a small group of Inspirationist young people who met for religious worship and were early supporters of Krausert's revival.

Unfortunately, Krausert proved to be a domineering leader unable to deal with the threats of religious persecution that his revival generated and the unwillingness of many older Inspirationists to accept his leadership. Conflict that erupted among the three leaders ended in 1819, with the leading elders of the sect ordering Krausert to leave. Metz ceased to speak in Inspiration, leaving Heinemann as the only *Werkzeug*. In 1823, tired of the demands placed upon her and anxious to have a normal life, Heinemann married Georg Landmann, a schoolteacher. The Inspirationists, who held celibacy to be the most pleasing to God, viewed Heinemann's marriage as a spiritual fall. Accordingly, Heinemann ceased to deliver testimonies. Christian Metz, who had once again begun to speak in Inspiration that winter, took her position and remained the group's charismatic leader for the next forty-four years.

Like the *Werkzeuge* who came before him, Metz made visitational journeys to the scattered congregations. In the early 1830s, he expanded his visits to include Inspirationist communities in Switzerland that had been largely ignored for several decades. Here, Metz led a revival.

During the 1820s and 1830s, civil authorities began to revoke privileges granted to the various Inspirationist communities and to question their rights to educate their own children and refuse military service. In 1826, Metz rented an abandoned convent in the liberal province of Hesse Darmstadt as a refuge for his followers. Members of some of the persecuted congregations gathered at the convent, Marienborn, and began to form a community life there. At the same time, Metz's testimonies began to suggest that:

> The time will come, and it is not far distant, when I [the Lord] will remove My luminaries [the Inspirationists] from there and put them in a different place. Eventually, I will gather all those who follow and remain true to Me. I will assemble them into . . . one flock.[4]

Over the next seven years, Metz and his associates leased additional properties as sanctuaries, including Herrnhaag in 1828, Arnsburg (which the Inspirationists renamed "Armenburg") in 1832, and Engelthal, also an abandoned convent, in 1834. Approximately three hundred to four hundred of the Inspirationist faithful ultimately congregated at these leased properties. Moving to the estates was a major commitment on the part of the faithful, as it required uprooting themselves from their homes and, in some cases, their homeland. They also had to forego private family homes when they moved into large common buildings with other Inspirationists.[5]

Although they continued to maintain their own money and property, certain aspects of the Inspirationist existence became communal while they were housed on the estates. Fields were tilled communally for the good of the community, and at Herrnhaag and Armenburg wealthier members of the Society established woolen factories to provide much-needed employment and income for the sect. Church leaders paid rents for the estates from a common fund, while income was divided among the members "according to their ability and time spent at work." Finally, meals and church services on the estates were held in large common rooms. Not only did the Inspirationists become used to living and working together during this time, but they also became used to submitting to the authority of the *Werkzeug* and other elders in secular as well as in spiritual matters. At the same time, Metz and the elders worked to unify the separate estate congregations through regular visits and through holding conferences for the elders of the four communities. Thus, by the late 1830s, the Inspirationists set the stage for the expansion of communal living that was to follow.[6]

Engelthal

Originally a Catholic convent—the name means "valley (or vale) of the angels"—this property was leased by the Inspirationists in 1834 as a refuge for members fleeing religious persecution elsewhere. This view is a hand-colored lithograph by Joseph Prestele, Sr. (1796–1867), circa 1840.

Top: *Middle Ebenezer, lithograph, circa 1850, by Joseph Prestele, Sr. The building in the center is the Middle Ebenezer meetinghouse. Logs in the millrace are being floated to the nearby sawmill.*

Below: *View of Lower Ebenezer, circa 1850. Unsigned watercolor, attributed to Friedrich "Fritz" Jeck (1821–1906). This view is from the village gristmill on Casenovia Creek, looking toward the main village. The frame building in the lower right was a kitchen house. The rest of the village was located on a rise, visible in the background.*

The Ebenezer Society

Then Samuel took a stone and set it up between Mizpah and Shen.
He named it Ebenezer, saying, "Thus far has the Lord helped us."
1 Samuel 7:12

In 1842, facing the effects of a long drought, increased rents, and continued persecution, Metz delivered a testimony directing the community to seek a home in the New World: "Your goal and your way shall lead towards the west to the land which still is open to you and your faith. . . ." Within a few weeks of this testimony, Metz and three associates boarded the ship *New York* and set sail across the Atlantic. After a stormy voyage, the committee arrived in New York and, after fruitless searches elsewhere, purchased a 5,000-acre tract on the Buffalo Creek Indian Reservation just outside the city of Buffalo, New York, from the Ogden Land Company. The new site was described by Wilhelm Noé in a letter back to the community in Germany:

> It rained all day, but we were very favorably impressed [with the land] . . . there is still considerable good timber a little ways distant. An Indian took us across the creek in a hollowed out tree trunk. Do not form any extravagant opinions about America. The county is still wild and no Germany. So forget any ideas, as some have already written, about pleasure walks under the walnut trees . . . but with united effort and love and unity it can be changed into a garden—the opportunity is here. It is a nice plain with small hills here and there. . . .[7]

Unfortunately for the Inspirationists, the Ogden Company did not yet possess clear title to the property, and it would be four years before such a title could be produced. In the meantime, the Inspirationist faithful began migrating to their new home.

In February 1843, before their co-religionists arrived, Metz and Wilhelm Noé crafted a "preliminary constitution" that may have reflected organizational discussions held in Germany. Under terms of the agreement, each member of the Society was to surrender his/her property to a common fund for a period of three years. The leaders agreed to use the fund to pay passage for poorer members of the sect, secure land, and otherwise fund development of the new settlement. Interest would accrue on funds deposited by the members, and the Society would provide them with food and shelter. After the three years had passed, the Society would redistribute its property among the members.[8]

Precisely why Metz chose to institute communal living at this point deserves some exploration. Perhaps the need for a large amount of money with which to purchase the contiguous tract of land led him to institute a common fund. The desire to assure that all members, regardless of their wealth, would be able to immigrate was likely also a factor. Metz would have been aware of the fact that such a system was not a significant departure from the arrangement previously held on the German estates, and so would prove acceptable to his followers. He may also have been motivated by a desire to emulate the first Christian church described in the book of Acts 2:44–45 in which all property was held in common: "All the believers were together and had everything in common. Selling their possessions and goods, they gave to anyone as he had need." Some historians have suggested that Metz's visit to the Zoar Communal Society in eastern Ohio the spring following his arrival may have cemented his thinking on the issue of communalism. Metz's scathing comments on that experience, however, suggest that—if anything—the visit may well have dampened his enthusiasm.

Metz named the new settlement "Ebenezer," a biblical term from 1 Samuel 7:12 meaning "thus far has the Lord helped us." The community legally became known as the "Ebenezer Society." Although not all Inspirationists emigrated, more than eight hundred of the faithful eventually undertook the forty-day sea voyage to the United States. Sailing on immigrant ships, the migrants faced long hours of boredom, sea sickness, spoiled food, and cramped accommodations.

Joseph Prestele, Sr., a church elder who sailed for Ebenezer in August 1843, wrote a letter to his father in Germany describing his experiences on board ship. In frail health prior to the voyage, Prestele had a particularly difficult experience. He noted, "I was so sick that I did not expect to live, and I was prepared to die. It was so despairing and hopeless. . . . This lasted the whole twenty-eight long days. I hardly had a good day, and I spent many sleepless nights. I cannot describe how endless they seemed. . . ."

Most of the Inspirationists landed at New York, then either boarded boats for the long trip across New York on the Erie Canal or, like Prestele, boarded trains. (For ninety-three-year-old Ulrich Murbach, the long voyage to the new settlement ended en route. Told not to make the long trip, Murbach insisted on coming anyway, only to expire while he and his family were aboard the train heading to Buffalo.) After traveling by canal boat and railroad to Buffalo, Prestele's company was met by men from Ebenezer with wagons to haul their possessions to the new settlement. Then the party began the final leg of their lengthy journey. Prestele described his joy at finally reaching his new home:

> We drove up a slight incline and when we were at the top there lay Ebenezer . . . before us. I was so surprised that they had built up so much already, but I was even more surprised when . . . the brother said to me, "this nice little house was built for you; you can move right in." I could hardly believe it, for all during the trip I had thought we would have to live in a log-cabin for at least a year. . . .[9]

Within a short time, the community had created three small villages on its New York land and acquired a large tract of Canadian land when its owner converted to the faith. By 1852 the community had created four villages in New York—Middle, Upper, Lower, and New Ebenezer—and two small outposts in Canada—Canada Ebenezer and Kenneberg. Each village was a self-sustaining unit with wagon and blacksmith shops, harness makers, cobblers, tinsmiths, and a pottery.

By 1846, a large woolen mill was operating at Middle Ebenezer, while tanneries, flour, and sawmills operated in the other villages. In the summer of 1847, a journalist wrote the following description of the community, one of the first ever published:

"In visiting this community, a stranger will not fail to be struck with the neatness, order, and perfection, with which all their farm operations are carried on; and the astonishing improvements they have made in so short a time—mostly within three years;—for, besides the buildings they have erected, they have cleared between 3,000 and 4,000 acres of land, from which nearly every stump is thoroughly eradicated, planted about 25,000 fruit trees, and made many miles of durable fences. Their gardens, yards and fields display refined taste and the highest state of cultivation; and from present appearances, they are destined to become immensely rich."[10]

Amana Heritage Society collection

Middle Ebenezer Woolen Mill,
photographed by Friedrich Oehl, 1901

Author's collection

Middle Ebenezer Brewery,
photographed by Peter Stuck, 1937

STATE OF NEW-YORK.

No. 243.

In Assembly,

March 4, 1845.

Reported by Mr. GARRETSON, from the committee on charitable and religious societies—read twice, and committed to the committee of the whole.

AN ACT

To incorporate "The Community of True Inspiration," in the county of Erie.

The People of the State of New-York, represented in Senate and Assembly, do enact as follows :

1 SECTION 1. George A. Weber, Christian Metz, Charles M. Winzenried,

2 Frederick Heineman, William Moerschel, Frederick Betz, Theobald Riec-

3 hert, Jacob Dorr, Theobald Heimburger, Benedict Gasser, Caspar Mur-

4 bach, Jacob Ruedy, Ernest Klein, Johannes Fink, Christian G. Ackermann,

5 and their associates, now composing the community of Germans, residing on

6 a part of the late Buffalo creek reservation, in the county of Erie, and all

7 persons who shall hereafter belong to such community, or the corporation

8 hereby created, shall be and they are hereby declared and constituted a

9 body politic and corporate, by the name of "The Community of True In-

10 spiration," with power by their corporate name to contract and be contracted

11 with, sue and be sued, implead and be impleaded, defend and be defended,

12 in all courts of law and equity in this state and elsewhere ; to have a com-

[No. 243.]   1

Original printed copy, collection of the author

Formal act of the New York State Legislature in 1845
giving legal recognition to the Ebenezer Society

As the community became established in its new home, Metz realized the need to formalize and extend his communal arrangement indefinitely. A permanent constitution was drawn up and signed by the members and, in 1846, the New York State Assembly formally incorporated the community as the "Community of True Inspiration." The constitution vested the leadership of the Society into the hands of a thirteen-member "Board of Trustees" known as the *Bruderrath* (Council of Brethren). Every adult male member of the Society and widowed or single female members over the age of thirty voted for the members of the *Bruderrath*. Once elected, trustees tended to serve for life.

By 1854 the Ebenezer villages had reached a state of settlement and organization beyond that of most rural communities of the time. Bound together by religion and their unique economic system, the Inspirationists were also in daily contact with one another, whether working side by side in the fields or in the kitchen houses. Such contact strengthened the growing bonds of community.

Yet, for the apparent strength of the Society, internal and external forces threatened its long-term survival. Internally, some divisions between community members were apparent. For example, in 1846 there was a debate on whether or not the community should observe total celibacy, during which Metz was openly challenged in a church service by a member who felt that he was not strict enough on this issue; it went away without serious harm. Other problems were more persistent and insidious. In what would prove the bane of the Inspirationists' communal experience, Society members realized they had no incentive to work particularly hard. Communal activity lessened demands on the individual worker, and deficiencies in one worker's efforts would be compensated for by those of another, leaving little motivation for personal initiative. As a result, by 1854 the Society already employed hired hands to perform certain tasks on its farms and mills, including workers with skills not already found among Society members.

Society records indicate a growing concern by Metz and other leaders over a developing sense of materialism and an indifference to spiritual teachings by members of the Society. Such a "falling away" from core principles was likely fueled by the fact that the nearby city of Buffalo possessed a large and vibrant German immigrant community with which Society members had some contact and whose lifestyle they likely envied. Explaining the situation in a letter to a German associate, Metz expressed particular concern for the impact of Buffalo on the Society's young: "We love . . . seclusion and privacy . . . and [Buffalo] is not a good influence on our young people."[11]

Externally, Society leaders were buffeted by attacks from competing business interests and hostile neighbors. In the spring of 1854, complaints that the Society failed to meet its fair share of the tax burden led to a formal investigation by a committee of the New York General Assembly. At the same time, a dispute involving a dam a few miles downstream from the villages threatened to draw the community into a lawsuit. The dam, originally constructed in 1828 by the Buffalo Hydraulic Association, diverted water from Buffalo Creek into a canal that powered several tanneries and other industries in the city of Buffalo. Over time the canal had silted in, leading the Association to raise the level of their dam on Buffalo Creek rather than dredge the canal bed. This action caused water to back up in the creek bed and flood some of the Inspirationists' low-lying fields. Worse still, the higher water level often made it impossible for the turbines of the Middle Ebenezer mills to function. The Association, alarmed by Inspirationist complaints about the dam, filed a formal court injunction, later overturned, against the Society. On the same day the injunction was filed, August 31, 1854, Christian Metz delivered an *Einsprache* (written, as opposed to spoken) testimony directing the Society to seek a new home in the West.[12]

Within days of Metz's testimony, the Inspirationists' organized a scouting party. The committee, including Metz, traveled to the new territory of Kansas in September 1854 but failed to locate or purchase a suitable tract. Plagued with illness and perhaps unsettled by the growing controversy over slavery in the territory, the committee returned to Ebenezer, along the way observing the wives of slaveholders in Missouri, whom Metz derided, stating that they were "dressed in silk and veils, and do no work. They sit at home in their rocking chairs and rock themselves!"[13]

Following the return of the Kansas expedition, Society leaders considered their next course of action, even consulting former president

Millard Fillmore, living in retirement in Buffalo, for advice. Fillmore, who had once served as legal counsel for the Society, provided them with a letter of recommendation, praising them as "most excellent citizens, quiet, peaceable, industrious and honest . . ." A second committee, presumably bearing Fillmore's letter, traveled to Iowa and located a tract of land on its first day of exploration only twenty miles from the then state capital in Iowa City. In June of 1855, a third committee began to purchase what would eventually amount to 26,000 acres of land in the heavily wooded valley of the Iowa River.[14]

A New Home in the Iowa River Valley

Photograph by Joan Liffring-Zug Bourret

This fish weir was constructed by Native Americans, possibly members of the Meskwaki tribe, on the Iowa River near the Amana village of Homestead around the seventeenth century. The weir, known locally as the "Indian Dam," is listed on the National Register of Historic Places. The floods of 1993 silted over the rocks and the "v" is no longer visible.

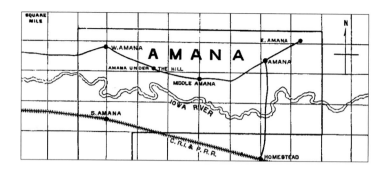

This map of the Amana villages was included in Charles Nordhoff's 1874 account of the community.

This 1874 engraving of the street leading toward the Amana Woolen Mill is one of the earliest dated images of the Amana villages. The tower at left contained the watch room, where lookouts sat at night to watch for signs of fire in the village. The woolen mill, the large building at the end of the street, was enlarged as the popularity of Amana woolens grew in subsequent years. With the exception of one house, all of the buildings visible in this engraving are still standing.

Life in Communal Amana

High Amana, view from the southeast, attributed to Joseph Prestele, Sr., circa 1860. This view enhanced an early map of the village.

Until 1932 the government of the Amana Society was vested in a board of thirteen elected trustees, collectively called the Grosse Bruderrath *("Great Council of the Brethren" or "Board of Trustees"). Qualified members of the Society voted for the trustees each December. Six of the members were elected at large, while each village was guaranteed at least one seat on the board. The* Bruderrath *met each month, alternating their meetings between the various villages. The room pictured here is where they held their meetings in Main Amana.*

Life in Communal Amana

Come with me from Lebanon, my bride, come with me from Lebanon. Descend from the crest of Amana, from the top of Senir, the summit of Hermon, from the lions' dens and the mountain haunts of the leopards.

Song of Songs 4:8

The new site in Iowa, unlike Ebenezer, was relatively isolated from the outside world. Additionally, the river and a large creek promised suitable waterpower, while the large stand of timber, clay, and stone outcroppings provided easily available building materials. Settlement began with the arrival of a hand-picked contingent of thirty-three settlers who left Ebenezer on July 9, 1855. This advance party began clearing land and constructing houses and barns at what became the village of Amana, a biblical name (Song of Solomon 4:8), chosen by Metz because of its meaning to "remain true." In the following year, more settlers arrived from Ebenezer, and a new settlement, West Amana, was started on the northwestern corner of the Society's landholdings.

Within seven years of arriving in Iowa and settling Amana, the Society started six new villages, spreading the communities across its estate roughly an hour apart by ox cart. As in Ebenezer, the villages were either named for their geographic location or for a physical feature: West Amana (1856), South Amana (1856), High Amana (1857), East Amana (1860), and Middle Amana (1862). The Society purchased the nearby village of Homestead in 1861 to gain access to the newly constructed Mississippi and Missouri (later Rock Island) Railroad.

Each village was surrounded by its own farm district averaging roughly 2,000 acres. As in Ebenezer, the Inspirationists farmed their new holdings in the open-field manner they had known in Germany—farm workers inhabited a village and worked the land surrounding it, but no one lived on an independent farmstead. The Inspirationists funded their Iowa purchases through the sale of their Ebenezer holdings, although the financial panic of 1857 temporarily halted land sales and forced the community to borrow large sums of money from Buffalo banks.

On December 30, 1864, the final contingent of settlers arrived at Amana from Ebenezer. By that time, the Amana villages had a population of 1,228 members.[15]

The 1860s were years of growth and development at Amana, as the community planted crops and built homes, barns, shops, and factories. Each village was laid out so that the *Saal*, or meetinghouse, was centrally located, with shops and barns at the edge of town. The most significant construction activity involved completion of a seven-mile-long millrace that diverted water from the Iowa River for use at the Society's various mills and factories. The millrace, begun in 1865, took four years to construct. The completed canal powered the Society's woolen mills, the Amana calico mill, machine shops at both Main and Middle Amana, a starch factory at Middle Amana, and a flour mill at Main Amana.

The millrace brought water seven miles from the Iowa River to power the factories of the villages. Men using oxen dug the canal. This view of the millrace, taken around 1900, shows the dredge boat that traveled up and down the canal each year to remove the silt that accumulated in the canal bed. The branch of the millrace to the right led to the Amana Calico Factory, shown in a 1903 photograph opposite page, top. Printed calico cloth was sold nationally until blue dye was unattainable from Germany during World War I. This part of the millrace was filled in during the 1940s.

The Calico Factory

The Amana Flour Mill

Photographed by Bertha M. H. Shambaugh in 1892, this flour mill and the calico factory were two of several with power supplied by the millrace. Other factories included the Amana and Middle Amana Woolen Mills and two machine shops.

STATE OF IOWA.

HEAD QUARTERS,

Provost Marshal's Office, 4th District.

IOWA CITY, NOVEMBER 25TH, 1863.

List of persons enrolled subject to MILITARY DUTY in the several Sub-Districts in the County of Iowa, State of Iowa, in pursuance of an Act of Congress, passed March 3rd 1863, and published herein as required by Circular No. 101, issued by Col. JAMES B. FRY, Provost Marshal General, Washington City, Nov. 17th, 1863.

IOWA COUNTY.

AMANA TOWNSHIP.

SUB-DISTRICT NO. 76.

CLASS NO. 1.

NAMES.	AGE.	NAMES.	AGE.	NAMES.	AGE.
Burgy, Christian	81	Rample, Genit J.	26	Roth, Henry	38
Burg, Henry	22	Jack, Frederick	42	Latzell, Carl	29
Berthart, Paul	21	Jack, Peter	35	Lind, Adam	30
Barringer, Christopher	98	Jack, Charles	33	Specht, Phillip	34
Bortz, John A.	27	Pitz, Jacob	31	Schofer, John	38
Bernhart, George	80	Koch, Theophilus	25	Slangnessy, Patrick	32
Buhler, John	36	Kariger, Peter	25	Siuener, Nicholas	38
Boyer Jacob	26	Kircher, Jacob	37	Specht, Julius	30
Brown, Alexander	28	Koch, John	43	Schnider, Carl	36
Brenema, Carl	40	Kibs, John	40	Siuener, Jacob	39
Berthart, Daniel	32	Kircher, John A.	31	Schmitzer, John	20
Binder, Andrew	33	Marbach, Jacob	41	Schneider, Jacob	37
Boyer, Henry	33	Marback, Adam	37	Stotz, William	36
Boyer, George	42	Marbach, Casper	44	Schiff, Andrew	28
Benhart, Alexander	21	Maas, Henry	36	Stuck, Jacob	26
Crausse, Charles	36	Moershall, Frederick	24	Tomtry, John	18
Ebbricht, Carl	32	Moershall, Charles	32 40	Stuck, Henry	30
Erzinger, John George	26	Mullen, Guslan	39	Schneider, George	27
Eisinger, George	29	Maas, Jacob	24	Schneider, Theophilus	26
Zschecker, Jacob	28	Maas, George	34	Noller George	36
Fritz, George	27	Pitz, William	33	Troutman, Lorenzo	33
Fritz, John	42 32	Pfeiffer, Caspar	31	Troutman, Charles	32
Fehr, Henry R.	31	Pitz, Peter	31	Urban, Andrew	
Flick, George	29	Pitz, Karl	28	Urban, John	
Feiba, Samuel	23	Pitter, Andrew	28	Wener, Gotheib	
Gopp, Adolph	27	Pitz, George	30	Wolf, Adolph	
Butler, John	28	Prestte, Theophilus	35	Wolff, Julius	

Author's collection

Broadside listing of men subject to military duty November 25, 1863. Most of the men on this list were members of the Amana Society. Eighteen Amana men were ultimately drafted for military service, but were exempted when the Society paid $300 commutation fees for each of them. A few members of the Society served in the war, but were not members at the time of their service.

The settlement of the Amana villages occurred during the American Civil War, an event that Society leaders, particularly Christian Metz, watched with trepidation. Because of their pacifistic religious views, the Society refused to take part in the conflict, paying commutation fees for the eighteen Amana men who were ultimately drafted. During the war, the Society made substantial contributions of clothing and money to soldiers' aid organizations, a practice of benevolent giving the Society continued to follow during natural disasters such as the San Francisco earthquake in 1906. During the months preceding the war and in the first two years of the conflict, Metz delivered six inspired testimonies directed at the government in Washington, particularly President Lincoln, which community members translated and sent to the president. The testimonies urged for a peaceful resolution to the conflict, but ceased shortly after Lincoln issued the Emancipation Proclamation, thus turning the war into a moral crusade against slavery.

Two years after the close of the Civil War, on July 24, 1867, Christian Metz, the beloved charismatic leader of the community, died at age seventy-two. Metz had been uniquely suited for his role as leader of the Society. A man of deep personal humility and piety, he was also a gifted administrator who knew when to compromise as well as when to stand firm. In 1947, Christine Christen, one of the last Amana residents with memories of Metz, left this recollection of the leader in an interview summarized by Alan DuVal in his 1948 Ph.D. dissertation about Metz:

> Christian Metz was described as being a sturdy, heavy-set man of medium height. He had straight brown hair and wore glasses. He was not stern or strict but frequently smiled and was pleasant in his attitude toward his associates. He was friendly towards all, and was highly respected. Everyone, including the children, would cross the street or go out of the way to greet him and shake his hand. He knew all the people by name and spoke pleasantly to them. Everyone found it easy to talk to him. He loved children and in turn children held a great affection for him. He was always humble and kind by disposition.[16]

Photograph by Joan Liffring-Zug Bourret

Middle Amana Cemetery

Each Amana village has its own cemetery in which members were, and are, buried in chronological order of death, with identical concrete markers. Both Christian Metz and Barbara Heinemann Landmann are buried in nondescript graves in the Main Amana cemetery.

Metz's mantle as *Werkzeug* fell upon Barbara Heinemann Landmann who had regained her gift of Inspiration in 1849 and who continued to spiritually guide the community until her death in 1883 at age eighty-eight. Landmann's gender, however, combined with what is reported as an abrasive personality, limited her actual leadership role within the community.

Living Communally

Daily life in communal Amana quickly settled into a familiar pattern that remained unchanged for more than seventy years. Children were cared for by their mothers until they reached the age of three, after which they spent part of each day in the village *Kinderschule*, or daycare. At age five, children entered one of the village schools, which followed the German *Volkschule* pattern of classroom instruction interspersed with manual training and playtime. During the *Arbeitsschule* periods of the day, special instructors taught the younger children to knit, while older children tended school gardens, helped tend the village onion field, assisted in a nearby kitchen house, or worked in the orchards. As one resident later remembered, "We school children had to trim the trees and pick the apples. There was no spray at that time, but we had to pick the apples, and they were distributed among the kitchens then."[17]

At age fourteen, Amana youth entered the work force. Boys often began work on the farm where most of the Society's labor force was employed. Later, the village elders might assign them to work in one of the Society's craft shops or in the woolen, calico, or flour mills. Girls were always assigned to work in one of the Society's more than fifty communal kitchens. Each kitchen, under the management of a *Küche Baas*, fed between twenty and forty community residents five times a day. Older women might spend a few hours at the kitchen house preparing vegetables for cooking or working in the enormous three-acre gardens that supplied each kitchen with vegetables, while younger women tended indoor labor. Elizabeth Schaedlich Dickel, who worked in two Middle Amana kitchens, remembered the system this way:

> There were three cooks. One cook cooked . . . [while] one [washed] the dishes and the other rinsed them and put them away. And then the next week, the dishwasher cooked and the cook before washed the dishes, and so on. There were other people who took care of the food . . . peeled potatoes and scraped the carrots and things like that. That usually was done in the evening, before.[18]

Bertha M. H. Shambaugh photographs

Top: *Amana school boys in apple orchard at Main Amana, circa 1892*
Below: *Interior of a kitchen house showing hearth and tin cooking implements, circa 1892*

*Group of workers at the Dittrich Kitchen House, Middle Amana, 1924
The young woman in white is the author's grandmother, Helene Hergert
Hoehnle, who was then seventeen.*

This photograph of children at the Middle Amana Kinderschule
*("children's school" or daycare) was taken by an unknown photographer
around 1905. The small* Kinderschule *building that these children
attended was restored in the 1970s by an Amana youth group and still
serves as a meeting place for local organizations.*

Male community members worked at any one of a variety of jobs. Each Amana village maintained many craft shops. The men who operated them—harness makers, blacksmiths, wheel and wagon makers, and others—maintained the equipment and animals needed on the village farms. Additionally, most Amana villages featured basket makers, cobblers, cabinet shops, general stores, locksmiths, carpet weavers, barrel makers, bakeries, and meat markets. A small number of tinsmiths, watchmakers, printers, book binders, tailors, and brewers operated in the larger villages.

In Main Amana, Upper and Lower South Amana, and Homestead, all of which had rail connections, large hotels served the needs of traveling salesmen and farm families who came to do business at the general stores. In Middle Amana and Main Amana, male community members staffed the Society's large woolen mills as well as the Amana calico mill.

Unlike the Old Order Amish, who shun modern technology, members of the Amana Society eagerly embraced modern conveniences that would expedite their work. The Amana Woolen Mill was lit by electric lights by the turn of the twentieth century, while the villages were connected by the Society's own telephone system, and Society-owned cars and trucks carried goods and services between the seven villages.

Visitors were quick to note the laid-back attitude Amana workers gave their jobs. After a visit to the Amana Woolen Mill, one observer commented, "The mill hands were not 'hurting themselves' by too much work, but looked placid and contented." From the Society's days at Ebenezer, outsiders commented that members simply did not work very hard, but still the products of their hands were honest and well-made. With the security provided by communal life, Amana residents lacked the incentive of earning a wage to drive their work habits.[20]

To carry some of the labor burden, the Society employed an increasing number of hired hands on its farms and in its factories. Largely unskilled, unmarried, and German-speaking, these *Taglöhner* or "day laborers" provided a window on the customs of the outside world for Society members. *Taglöhner* lived in little houses near the edge of each village, many staying for decades and a few even marrying Amana women or joining the Society.

Homestead baker John Beck, Sr. (1879–1932) poses by his dough trough in this circa 1915 photograph. The baker set the dough for each day's baking out in the rye-straw baskets visible on the two tables to the right.

Although they did not receive wages for their work, each adult member of the Society received a line of credit at the village's general store. Couples with children received a set amount per child to buy such things as shoes, fabric for making clothes, candy, tea, sugar, and other sundries. Each single person or family had their own credit book, which they presented when making purchases or at any of the craft shops to cover the expenses of such things as repairing a bucket. The Society provided food, shelter, and fuel to each member without cost. The allowances, which varied over time, limited consumption by Society members and also assured that no one received more than their fair share of goods or services. Church elders reprimanded individuals who overdrew their credit allowance, while those who did not overspend were allowed to carry any remaining balance over to the next year at the general stores in each village.

The two pictures on the opposite page, by West Amana photographer Rudolph Kellenberger, are of the lengthy process of producing hay for that village's livestock. The bottom photograph, by Peter Stuck, shows a Main Amana crew threshing grain in the 1920s.

Horses to Tractor Power

Top: *Each village had numerous craftsmen, such as Main Amana blacksmiths Carl Ackermann (1894–1961) and Henry Schumacher (1894–1958).*

Below: *Main Amana woodworker and cooper Carl Christen (1907–1968). Other craftsmen in Amana villages included broom makers, cobblers, harness makers, tinsmiths, wagon makers, wheelwrights, carpenters, carpet weavers, basket weavers, and bakers.*

Left: *West Amana farm scenes by Rudolph Kellenberger (1907-1996) show the farm crew hauling sand back to their village, shown in the background of the top photo. The middle and bottom photos confirm that the Amana farms were quick to adopt new equipment, including tractors and a steam engine.*

Above: *A prominent feature in the Amana landscape is Lily Lake, located between Main and Middle Amana. Each year, thousands of American lotus lilies cover the lake from late July until early August. This picture, taken by Peter Stuck in 1927, shows men seining the lake for carp.*

Below: *Rudolph Kellenberger took this photograph of the West Amana farm crew cutting ice on the Iowa River in the 1930s. Each village had at least one large icehouse where ice was stored all summer long for use in the iceboxes that were features of each communal kitchen.*

Not all Amana men worked on the farms or in craft shops. In Main and Middle Amana, several dozen Amana men and women operated the Society's two woolen mills and calico mill. The top photograph shows Amana Woolen Mill workers in December 1899. The photo below, taken by Peter Stuck in 1928, shows the mill's spinning department.

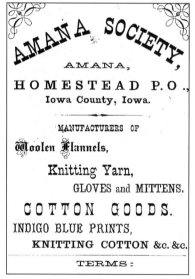

The Amana Society marketed the products of its woolen, flour, and calico mills across the country. Shown here are a circa 1900 advertisement for Amana rye flour, an 1877 catalogue for woolen and calico products, and a sack used to pack products of the West Amana Flour Mill.

Religious Life

Beyond their workaday life, Amana residents attended eleven church services each week, including an *Nachtgebet* (evening prayer service) each evening, and services during the day on Wednesday and Saturday and twice on Sunday. Although the brief *Nachtgebet* services were generally held in designated residences, the weekend services were held in the village *Versaamlungsaal*, a large, centrally located brick or sandstone building. Inside the *Saal*, men sat on one side and women on the other facing a bench of elders who conducted the service. Worship consisted of readings from the Bible as well as from the inspired testimonies of the *Werkzeuge*, *a cappella* hymns sung from the *Psalter-Spiel*, and prayer.

This early 1900s view of Main Amana shows a group of school girls on their way to a church service. The tower visible on the frame house contained the village bell, which was rung to signal the start and end of the workday, the afternoon meal, and an emergency such as a fire. Every Sunday at 8 a.m., it was rung for residents to set their watches and clocks to the correct time.

Exterior of the Main Amana meetinghouse, circa 1892, Bertha M. H. Shambaugh, photographer. Built in 1864, this building continues to serve as a place of worship for the Amana community.

Joan Liffring-Zug Bourret photograph

Interior of the Homestead meetinghouse, 1960s. Although they differed in size, the interiors of each Amana village meetinghouse were very similar. Last used for active worship in 1990, the Homestead meetinghouse is now an Amana Heritage Society museum site.

In 1914, Henry Wallace, later secretary of agriculture and vice president under Franklin Roosevelt, spent several days visiting and observing the Amanas. He left this rare account of a communal-era church service from an outsider's perspective:

> The congregation was, for the most part, clad in plain black. Everyone carried two big books, one the [P]salter-[S]piel or hymnal, and the other the Bible. For the first five or ten minutes [they] . . . seemed to be engaged in silent prayer. And then . . . the presiding elder, announced [a] hymn. . . . Then . . . the congregation began to sing, and such music I never heard before. It was very slow and majestic. . . . After beginning, the music never once stopped. . . . The blending of the men's and women's voices in the singing of the old German hymn . . . was so beautiful yet sad that I felt truly religious. . . . How they managed to sing so well without an instrument of any kind was a mystery to me. . . . Before praying, everyone kneeled, and each member of the congregation offered up a prayer. . . . There was more singing, and then the fifteenth chapter of John was read, each member taking a verse. The whole service was of course in German, and I could do no more than catch the general drift of it. . . . At the close, the . . . [congregation] . . . marched out . . . everyone in this way getting out of the church "decently and in order."[21]

Many special services punctuated the Amana church calendar. Beyond observances of traditional Christian holidays such as Christmas, Holy Week, Good Friday, Easter, and Ascension Day, church members observed several unique services. Each year community members gathered for the annual *Unterredung*, at which they publicly declared the sins they had committed that year. On Thanksgiving Day, each village congregation observed the *Bundesschliessung*, or covenant renewal service, during which members reaffirmed their religious covenant with God and the church by shaking the hands of the elders.

The most important religious service was the biannual *Liebesmahl*, or Communion service. This service was held in the large meetinghouse in Main Amana, a building specially designed for the purpose, with wooden partitions that could be removed to expand the main sanctuary to accommodate members from other villages. *Liebesmahl* was held over a period of several days. During the first service, the members of the *Erste Versammlung* (the first church, usually consisting of the oldest members in each village) met, and as part of their worship engaged in foot washing, as Jesus did during the last supper. After a dinner hour, the congregation reconvened and partook of sacramental wine and bread while seated around long wooden tables, which were formed by placing the partition panels on specially constructed sawhorses. Services on subsequent days involved the members of the *zweite* (second, mainly middle-aged) and *dritte* (third, mainly young adult) congregations from each village. The elders in each village held special Communion services for young children at kitchen houses, during which hot chocolate and coffee cake were substituted for the usual bread and wine.

Although the church encouraged members to remain celibate, the majority, 87 percent, of the total adult membership eventually married. Prospective couples had to make their intentions known to the *Bruderrath*, which then approved the marriage and specified a waiting period, usually a full year, before the ceremony would take place. Although practices gradually loosened over time, the prospective bridegroom was often sent to live in another village during this enforced engagement, and visits between the prospective couple were limited and supervised. At the end of the year, the wedding took place before a small congregation of friends and family, followed by a celebration at a local communal kitchen. Three weeks after the wedding, the elders assigned living quarters to the couple, often in the same home as the bride's parents.

*This formal portrait of Marie Therese (1847–1910) and Heinrich Stuck
(1832–1891) depicts the couple wearing their church attire. Although
church leaders frowned upon photographs as graven images, many Amana
people had studio portraits taken while visiting neighboring communities,
such as Iowa City, where a photographer in the Townsend Gallery took this
picture of the Stucks around 1885.*

Home and Family Life

Most Amana homes were occupied by multiple generations of the same extended family. Homes were large, built of brick, sandstone, or wood, and featured fifteen-foot square rooms separated by wide hallways for privacy. Because cooking occurred only in kitchen houses, most residences consisted only of a succession of sleeping rooms and parlors. If conditions within the home became crowded, the family could ask the elders to relocate them to another house. When a kitchen boss became too old to perform her duties, the elders gave charge of her kitchen to a younger woman, who would then move into the house with her family. Other individuals who happened to live in the same building as their shop could also be moved when they were replaced due to age or infirmity. As one resident recalled, "My Grandpa . . . he was a baker back then. Then he couldn't bake anymore . . . [so] we had to move. They just moved you from one place to another because you didn't own the house." The exteriors of Amana houses were covered with wooden trellises, covered with climbing grapevines. The vines shaded the buildings and helped keep them cool during the summer, while the grapes contributed to the community's stock of preserves and wine.[22]

Distinctive features of Amana houses included nine-over-six-pane window sashes, return gables, and symmetrical windows and doors. Many of these features were copied from Greek Revival and Federal houses that the Inspirationists observed while living at Ebenezer, New York, and do not reflect German architecture.

Left, top: *Peter Stuck took this portrait of his aunt, Lina Trautmann, in her Main Amana apartment, circa 1928. The rag carpeting, table, and couch are typical Amana features, though the embroidered pillows demonstrate the lessening of restrictions by church elders on artistic self-expression after 1900.*

Below: *Residence of Dr. William Moershel (1865–1931), Homestead, Iowa, circa 1895. Like his son, Henry, after him, the Society sent Dr. Moershel to the State University of Iowa for his medical training, paying all expenses. The grape trellis, nine-over-six windows, and planter or* rabatt *around the foundation are typical Amana building features.*

Until well into the early twentieth century, Amana women, particularly the elderly, wore a cap, shawl, and apron as part of their daily attire. Later, this clothing was worn only to church services as a sign of humility, a practice that many Amana women still observe. Pictured above in this circa 1895 portrait are Jacob Selzer, Sr. (1863–1920), his sons Louis (1889–1960) and Jacob F. (1888–1917), and his wife, Louise Geiger Selzer (1863–1940), seated at left. The older women include Mrs. Selzer's mother, Louise Schnaebele Geiger (1841–1927), and three of her aunts.

The heavy timber framing, preference for stonework, and such features as mud and straw nogging, or insulation, in wooden houses reflect traditional German practices. The Society opened quarries for cutting sandstone at Main, Middle, High, and West Amana and used this soft stone to build the first woolen mill, homes, and meetinghouses, as well as the foundations of barns and other structures.

When first removed from the ground, sandstone is wet and soft, making it easy to shape. Workers would lay the stone in a field to cure for several months before using it in construction. The Society developed brickyards at Main, Middle, and South Amana and at Homestead. Bricks were stacked to create long tunnels. Workers kept wood fires inside the tunnels burning for over a week to fire the bricks.

Visitors to the Amana villages during the communal period often commented on the fact that the wooden buildings were unpainted. This practice reflected the belief of community leaders that paint was too expensive and that rotted or broken siding could easily be replaced. Streets throughout the villages were lined with wooden fences whose main purpose was to keep the livestock—which was periodically driven through town—from wandering into yards. Kerosene lanterns atop tall poles provided illumination at night for residents who walked to and from communal kitchens and church services along wooden foot paths.

Amana residents had plenty of free time to pursue various hobbies such as handwork, furniture making, and even fine art. Although church leaders frowned on decorative art as "worldly," most Amana women produced fine needlework, including house blessings that, because of their religious nature, were acceptable. Women also added decoration to such mundane items as match holders, newspaper racks, and pillow cases. Some women braided colorful throw rugs, knit fine doilies and table cloths, and sewed intricate designs into the otherwise plain quilts given to each newly married Amana couple.

Left, below: *Henry and Louise Miller enjoy a homemade rocking horse, circa 1915. Their father, F. William Miller, the Main Amana pharmacist, took the photograph. Louise and Henry were among the descendants of Christian Metz's only child, Anna Marie Kramer. Amana people made many of the toys given to their children at Christmas.*

West Amana photographer Paul Kellenberger (1909–2003) took this portrait of his neighbor, Carl Flick (1904–1976), at work in his home in 1937.

Work in the kitchens was often monotonous, hot, and difficult, but many women, when interviewed about their experiences for the Amana Heritage Society oral history project in later years, expressed fond memories of the kitchens. Most appreciated the camaraderie of working with other women, though the work itself was not enlivening. One woman remarked, "I think what bothered me more, was not like the work in the kitchen, but the sameness. You knew exactly on Monday what you were going to do all week. You even knew the menu, usually. . . ."[19]

Peter Stuck photograph

Making apple butter at the Noé Kitchen House, September 6, 1928, "Kitchen Boss" Louise Herrmann Noé (1879–1965) has her back to the camera. The Noé Kitchen now serves as the reception area of the Amana Heritage Museum.

Although the elders frowned upon visual arts such as photography and painting as violations of the second commandment prohibition on graven images, these arts thrived in later years as religious austerity lessened. Several Amana residents bought cameras and their work, together with the photography of Bertha M. H. Shambaugh, a gifted amateur photographer from Iowa City, forms an important chronicle of communal life. Notable exceptions to the early prohibition against representational art are the botanical illustrations produced by Joseph Prestele, trained as a lithographer in Germany, and his family for nursery companies and the Smithsonian Institution. The Presteles have received scholarly attention in recent years, as has the work of West Amana painter Carl Flick. Also noted is wood worker Friedrich Hahn of Middle Amana, who, in addition to making more than forty clocks, constructed a telephone system that linked the Amana villages by 1881.

Grant Wood Sketches in Amana

Peter Stuck took this photograph of Cedar Rapids artist Grant Wood (1891–1942) painting an oil sketch of the Stuck home in Main Amana in October 1927. Wood, who later gained international fame with his painting American Gothic, *was a frequent visitor to the Amana villages, where he befriended local artist Carl Flick and urged residents to maintain their traditional handcrafts and landscape at a time when such features were not valued within the community.*

William Noé, long-time Amana photographer, took this photograph of his brother, John (1900–1954), at work painting in the late 1940s.
Self-taught, John Noé began painting after the end of the communal system. His depictions of Amana scenes and Iowa barns and landscapes garnered him numerous awards before his untimely death.

East Amana resident Lina Bahndorf Trumpold (1868–1945) is shown removing walnut nutmeats in this 1939 portrait by William Noé.

Life in Amana was sedate and simple; the villages, resembling German *Dörfer* (villages), were noted for their profusion of flowers and gardens, which led one visitor to comment on "the large number of beautiful, old-fashioned flowers surrounding nearly every dwelling. An American child suddenly transported into an Amana village could imagine itself in fairyland." Demographically, 84 percent of the people who ultimately lived in the Amana Society came from central Germany, with an additional 7 percent from the province of Alsace (now part of France) and nearly 10 percent from Switzerland. German remained the principal language throughout the communal period, and German cultural traditions, such as Christmas trees, persisted among the otherwise austere Inspirationists.[23]

Members worked at their jobs as long as they were physically able. In many cases men unable to perform heavy physical labor were assigned by the village elders to perform lighter tasks such as weaving carpets or baskets. Older women prepared vegetables at the kitchen houses or cared for young children.

Johanna Müller (1860–1938) and Caspar Grimm (1841–1925), both of Main Amana, sat for these portraits by F. William Miller, circa 1917.

When death came, the village carpenter arrived at the home of the deceased to measure the body for a coffin. Friends and relatives came to the house to pay their respects. The funeral service was held at the main village meetinghouse. Then the congregation walked to the home of the deceased, where the coffin, which had remained at the house, was loaded on a light farm wagon and driven to the cemetery, with the members of the congregation following in a double row behind. At the cemetery, the deceased was laid to rest in the next available space and the grave marked with a simple concrete marker bearing the name, date of death, and age.

Although life in Amana was relatively peaceful, it was not without its moments of drama or interest. Major fires in both 1874 and 1881 destroyed the Middle Amana Woolen Mill, which was then rebuilt. In 1875 a large meteorite, known as both "The Amana Meteor" and the "Homestead Meteor" fell across the Amana Society lands. The largest fragment of this meteor, weighing 74 pounds, was the sixth-largest known piece of meteorite in the world at the time of its discovery.

On March 21, 1905, a mentally deranged man derailed the Rock Mountain Limited near Homestead, causing serious damage but resulting in only one death.

Finally, during the 1920s, Iowa archaeologists came to appreciate the prehistory of the Amana area as they noted the existence of several prehistoric earthworks, as well as a rare weir used to trap fish on the Iowa River and the bones of a prehistoric mastodon near the village of Amana.

Beyond natural disasters, the worst crises faced by the Society resulted from attacks by outsiders, including a 1905 lawsuit brought by the widow of the Iowa County attorney that charged that the Society had exceeded its charter as a religious organization by engaging in manufacturing. In a landmark 1906 ruling, the Iowa Supreme Court upheld the Society's right to exist, stating that the farms and manufacturing of the Society were not only provided for in its constitution, but also reflected the religious ideals of the community as it allowed members to lead an unselfish life, devoted to their religious beliefs.

In a ringing passage, the Court proclaimed:

> Under the blessings of free government, every citizen should be permitted to pursue that mode of life which is dictated by his own conscience, and if this, also, be exacted by an essential dogma or doctrine of his religion, a corporation organized to enable him to meet the requirement of his faith is a religious corporation and as such may own property and carry on enterprises appropriate to the object of its creation.[24]

The Society's pacifistic stance and German heritage made it a target of further attacks during World War I. Although more than twenty-five Amana men served in noncombatant capacity during the conflict, the Society invested thousands of dollars in war bonds, contributed to wartime scrap drives, and devoted its mills to government contracts, charges of disloyalty were still made. The editor of the nearby *Marengo Sentinel,* who referred to the Society as "but a clog on the wheel of progress," that was "not worth a damn to Iowa county nor to the State of Iowa," called for court action against "the Amana slackers" and suggested that it was the duty of the local community to "sweep the whole unwholesome mass [of Amana] into the Iowa River with a stub broom," or, perhaps more effectively, "knock the darn colony higher than the scaffold of Hamen."

Anti-German hostility was so strong nationwide that "sauerkraut" was known as "liberty cabbage" and even "German measles" were renamed "liberty measles."[25]

For almost eighty years, the Amana Society lay peacefully in the valley of the Iowa River, its members quietly pursuing their chosen way of life. The towering smokestacks of the Society's three factories cast shadows over the acres of cultivated fields, gardens, and flower beds. Life in Amana was never an idyllic Eden, but for those who remained within the community, life was unhurried and free of at least some of the cares faced by their counterparts in the world beyond their borders. As one resident noted in later years, "Communal living gave you the assurance that there was no need for you to be concerned about your livelihood. You were cared for."

A South Amana woman echoed these sentiments when she remarked, "When you were done, you were done. You didn't have [any] worry; you didn't have to worry where the money came from [to] buy something to eat or clothes. You got everything. You didn't have to worry about anything."[26]

Soon, however, the changes wrought by modern life in the outside world would place new pressures on the old Amana way, and the security of the communal era would be a thing of the past.

Opposite: *F. William Miller produced this patriotic portrait of his daughter, Louise Miller [DuVal] (1914–2002), left, and her friend, Lina Roth [Unglenk], during World War I. Like many other Pietist and Anabaptist groups, the Inspirationists were ardent pacifists. Prior to World War II, Amana men only served in noncombatant capacities in wartime, while the Society contributed to the Red Cross and other aid organizations. Since that time, many Amana residents have served in the military; the church has left the decision to the individual.*

Above: *Visitors to the Amana villages enjoy boating on the millrace in this early 1900s photograph. The woolen mill and flour mill are in the background. From the very early years of the Amana Colonies in Iowa, visitors came to see the seven villages.*

Right: *Visitors, including salesmen, could stay overnight in one of the Society's four hotels. The presence of these visitors, as well as the influence of the surrounding world, disastrous fires, and the Great Depression, were among the reasons why the Amana people voted to change their economic but not their religious life in 1932.*

Horses and Buggies to Motor Vehicles

A Coming Change

"The first generation has an idea and lives for that idea. The second generation perpetuates that idea for the sake of their fathers, but their hearts are not in it. The third generation openly rebels against the task of mere perpetuation of institutions founded by their grandfathers—it is always the same with people."

—F. William Miller, Main Amana pharmacist, 1933[27]

*Lights **On** in the Amanas*

Louis (1860–1938) and Marie Christen (1869–1955) Krauss, Amana, Iowa, reading by electric light, 1938. Photograph by William F. Noé. Louis Krauss came to the Society with his parents in 1867. Louis and Marie left the Society at the time of their marriage and lived outside from 1888 until 1890, when they returned.

In 1918, while the Society was still riding the crest of wartime production profits, its attorney recommended an amendment to the constitution that would provide for the dissolution of the communal organization. That such dissolution was necessary became apparent to many leaders during the 1920s, as both the textile industry and agriculture declined following the removal of wartime price supports in 1919. Society finances were further damaged by a major fire on August 11, 1923, that destroyed the Amana flour mill and much of the adjacent woolen mill that, although uninsured, was rebuilt.

Shortly after the August 11, 1923, fire that destroyed the Amana flour and woolen mills, Amana pharmacist F. William Miller took this photograph of residents surveying the damage. The ruins behind the men are of the woolen mill, of which only one major building, the weaving department, remained standing after the fire.

By 1932, the Society's total debt reached almost $500,000. At the same time, other problems, such as waste, corruption, an ongoing youth rebellion, and the $60,000 annually paid to hired workers, steadily eroded the Society's strength. Additionally, the Society had been without a charismatic leader since Landmann's death in 1883, and while the elders had been successful in managing the Society since that time, they had failed to adapt the communal system established under the guidance of the *Werkzeuge* to modern conditions.[28]

During the 1920s, the Society's religious values eroded as its youth, in particular, flaunted the old rules. Young men played baseball despite the warnings of the village elders, young girls had their hair cut short in fashionable "bobs," and residents used hoarded stashes of money gained through selling handwork and garden produce to outsiders to buy radios, magazines, and newspapers. As time went on, the elders permitted more and more of these activities, so that life in communal Amana began to resemble life elsewhere in rural Iowa of the 1920s. Even baseball became acceptable, as one young woman recounted in later years: "Saturday was always the boys' ball time. . . . That was something special. Our kitchen boss was really good and she said, 'Ja, you can stay. I'll start the cooking tonight. You just stay till the ball game is over.' " One of these baseball rebels, Bill Zuber, later became a pitcher for the New York Yankees.

Young people, dissatisfied with communal life, left the community in growing numbers. As one resident remembered, "I know in West Amana . . . as soon as they were out of school, they said, 'We're not going to stay here and work in the kitchens. We're going to leave . . .' [and] they did." Even without the economic problems of the early 1930s, it was clear that the Amana Society was falling apart at the seams by 1931.[29]

Following a lobbying effort by a group of concerned Amana men, the *Bruderrath* appointed a committee of four—Peter Zimmermann, manager of the Main Amana Woolen Mill, member of the Board of Trustees, and a church elder; Gustav Miller, manager of the West Amana Store; Adolph Heinemann, a bookkeeper and traveling salesman for the Society; and Dr. Charles Noé—to address members in each village and to explain the organization's precarious financial state. After these presentations in April 1931, Society members elected a committee to plan for the Society's future. Almost from the start, the "Committee of Forty-Seven," as it became known, began to plan for a complete reorganization of the Amana Society. In June they sent a formal letter and questionnaire to each adult member of the Society, asking whether they would be willing to return to a life of self-denial, or whether they would prefer reorganization. The membership voted 74 percent in favor of pursuing reorganization, with virtually all of the opposition coming from the village of Middle Amana.

The reason for Middle Amana's vote is complicated and a matter of debate. In 1931 the village was under the leadership of a beloved but conservative trustee who openly opposed reorganization, and villagers may have been persuaded by him. In addition, residents today suggest that a rumor circulated that outside interests were behind the push for reorganization in an attempt to seize the Society's assets. Middle Amana, unlike Homestead and Main Amana, where support for reorganization was high, was relatively isolated and unexposed to the visitors who shopped in the general stores, stayed in the hotels, or came to those villages on the railroads that stopped in each. Finally, circumstantial evidence suggests a campaign by Middle Amana village leaders to discredit the reorganization movement.[30]

Sind Sie damit einverstanden, daß der vorge-schlagene Plan, die Amana Society zu reorganisie-ren, welcher Ihnen kürzlich zur Durchsicht vorgelegt wurde, angenommen und ausgeführt wird?

☐ Ja

☐ Nein

This ballot was used by members of the Amana Society when they voted on reorganization, February 1, 1932. Translated it reads: "Do you agree that the plan to reorganize the Amana Society, as presented, should be adopted and followed?"

After months of deliberation, the committee produced a reorganization plan to create a joint stock business corporation, to retain the name "Amana Society," which would control the business aspects of the Society. A separate organization, the Amana Church Society, would oversee religious affairs. The plan provided for distribution of voting shares to adult members, entitling them to vote in Society elections and to receive medical and burial benefits from the new corporation. Additionally, the Society would issue prior distributive shares to each new member based on his or her years of service under the old system. Thus, an elderly member of the Society would receive stock shares representing his or her lifetime of service that could be redeemed for cash or credit at the Society's main office. The new plan also provided for the orderly appraisal of Society property and guaranteed members the right to purchase their homes. The plan was approved by 96 percent of the members when submitted for a vote on February 1, 1932.[31]

During the weeks that followed approval of the plan, the Society began a period of transition. In March and April, appraisers descended on the villages, and surveyors laid out lot lines where none had been before. The appraisers reviewed the equipment and inventory of each of the Society's 162 shops—not including the Society's woolen mills, four hotels, grain elevators, and farm departments, which were appraised separately.

The first significant shift in Society habits brought by the impending reorganization was when the communal kitchens served their last meal on the night of April 11, 1932. Fifty years later, Minnie Setzer of South Amana still lamented the end of the kitchen houses where she had worked for more than thirty years: "I missed the kitchens and the girls I worked with. Sure, it was easier to cook for my husband and myself instead of [for] thirty people, but I missed the girls in the kitchen." Marie Stuck, sixteen when the kitchens closed, reacted differently. "I thought it was kind of exciting for us when they changed over because we were getting kind of tired of working in the kitchens, so we thought that was a great thing." That fall, Stuck took advantage of her new-found freedom and started attending high school in a nearby community.[32]

In the weeks following the closing of the kitchens, the Society held auctions and sales in each of the seven villages so residents could purchase utensils with which to set up housekeeping. Most residents bought things

As part of the reorganization, the contents of the Amana kitchen houses were inventoried and sold at auction. Rudolph Kellenberger took this, and several other photographs, of the April 1932 auctions held in his hometown of West Amana.

for their sentimental value; few saw uses for the old lapboards, giant copper boilers, and oversized frying pans.

In April the Society's new business manager, a former bank examiner from Cedar Rapids, Arthur Barlow, arrived to assume his duties. Assisted by a hastily assembled staff, Barlow began to institute double-entry bookkeeping among the Society businesses. Barlow directed the closure of shops the Society deemed unprofitable. Individuals who worked in those shops were told that they could purchase their equipment and continue as a private business or take a new job within the Society.

The new organization guaranteed jobs to all of its members, which usually meant working in one of the factories or on the farm. For many craftspeople the change was minimal, since most had worked on the farms in the summer months anyway. Some craftsmen continued to operate their businesses as a sideline while working on the farm or in one of the factories. Carl Hergert, the Middle Amana cobbler, found work in the woolen mill after the reorganization but continued to repair shoes until the 1950s, while Phillip Griess continued to make brooms for his West Amana neighbors well into the 1960s.

Fifty Years After the Great Change

Amana residents remembered the change from religious communal life to free enterprise at a gathering on the grounds of the Museum of Amana History in 1982. Pictured at top are Arthur Barlow (1892–1983), right, who directed the change as the first business manager of the Amana Society, with Fred Blechschmidt of East Amana (1901–1987), member of the Committee of Forty-Seven, which planned the Great Change.

After the Great Change

Geh Aus, Mein Herz, Und Suche Freud

Go forth, my heart and seek delight
In all the gifts of God's great might,
These pleasant summer hours;
Look how the plains for thee and me
Have decked themselves most fair to see,
All bright and sweet with blossoms . . .

—Paul Gerhardt, 1659
Amana *Psalter-Spiel*
Translation by Catherine Winkworth, 1855

The Maxwell Automobile, above, was driven by Dr. William Moershel, Sr. The village doctors were among the first in the Amana villages to drive cars, which were owned by the Amana Society. Private ownership of vehicles came after the Great Change in 1932.

The Homestead Gas Station, below, is shown in a picture taken May 21, 1933, just a few months after the station opened.

74—

Amana Since 1932

"Perhaps out of the new Amana—with its undefined synthesis of capitalism, communism, and individualism, its greater freedom of initiative in meeting life's problems, its greater freedom of conscience in matters of religion and worship, and its innate love for the Good Life—there may emerge a community which [people] will some day write about and call Amana the Community of New Inspiration."

—Bertha M. H. Shambaugh, 1936[33]

On May 2, 1932, the new Amana Society Corporation came into existence and, for the first time, Amana workers were put on a payroll. The reorganization plan called for a transition period during which the Society and its members could adjust to the new order of affairs, and during which every worker, from the managers down to the farm hands, would receive ten cents an hour wage. To compensate for the low wage, the Society sold groceries and other items in their stores at cost to members.

Amana residents relished their new-found economic freedom. A Homestead farm worker remembered, "After the Change, we all went on the payroll. Ten cents an hour . . . We still worked until six in the evening . . . six days a week, so pay was not the biggest thing in our lives, although it bought our groceries and we were able to move ahead, buy an automobile . . . spend a little more money going to a picture show or things like that."[34]

Many Amana residents, when asked about the Great Change on its fiftieth anniversary, described it in positive terms. One resident, sixteen at the time of reorganization, commented, "I don't see how they could have lived any longer the way they did. . . . it just wouldn't have worked. [The reorganization] absolutely had to be. . . . [y]ou have to go forward, not backward, and this was a backward way of living."

Other residents recalled the anticipation of buying a car or of having their own kitchen. Some women expressed relief at being freed from the authority of their kitchen boss and the regimentation of kitchen life. In a demonstration of her new independence, one Amana woman served canned pineapple—something unheard of in the communal kitchens—at the first meal she prepared after the kitchens closed.

The individuals who were alive at the time of the anniversary, however, were young in 1932 and, as a result, their memories reflected the attitude of the Society's youth. For older residents, the Change was greeted with trepidation. One older High Amana woman, upset that she could no longer continue peeling potatoes at her kitchen house, which had allowed her to socialize, commented, "I cannot understand how those people who brought this [reorganization] on will be able to rest in their graves."[35]

The elderly woman who lamented the loss of her kitchen house job likely did not enter the post-communal workforce. Many younger women did, however. Amana women found wage labor jobs following the reorganization, one assumes in part because their income was needed at home, and also because they were used to working and wanted to preserve the camaraderie of their kitchen house experiences. Some women found work in the woolen mills. As late as 1936 the Society employed other women to maintain some of the kitchen gardens as small truck farming operations. Many women participated in the Society's short-lived attempts at producing mittens and canned goods for sale, known as "Department W." Still others helped sort and process seed corn the Society grew on special plots for the Pioneer Seed Corn Company, which was just starting to sell the hybrid corn varieties that would soon revolutionize agriculture.[36]

For men, the reorganization meant little change in their ordinary work habits. Most continued to work at the job they had done before the reorganization, provided they were employed by one of the sixty businesses that survived Barlow's purge. One difference that was frequently commented upon in later years was that many men who had professed illness, such as back trouble and an inability to work, before the reorganization suddenly "recovered" after it occurred. As one man recounted, "That was Barlow . . . they always said he was a good doctor." Residents attribute this shift to the realization that if they wanted their families to survive they would need to work. These miraculous cures led the colonists to bestow the nickname "Dr. Barlow" on their new business manager.[37]

Amana young people, many of whom had been part of the Society workforce since the age of fourteen, jumped at the opportunity to attend high school. Suddenly, young Amana men and women, who had been "adults" under the old Amana Society, found themselves once again immersed in youth culture and irresponsibility. Although these young people had to attend high school in neighboring communities, the newly formed Amana Community School District quickly revised the old communal educational system and opened a high school of its own in 1934. In 1954 the district opened a new elementary school building in Middle Amana to serve children of all seven villages. Later additions to this building expanded the facility to include the junior and senior high schools. In 1990, due to declining enrollment and threat of funding cuts, the district began the process of merging with a neighboring district. Both districts maintain their original elementary facilities, use the rest of the Amana facility for a combined junior high, and share a high school building in the nearby community of Tiffin.

Left: *William Noé photographed these Homestead women sorting seed corn in 1937.*

During the 1930s, the Amana Society managed to show a modest profit at the end of each year. The employment and stock structures created by the reorganization proved to be effective. Still, the Amana Society remained much as it had always been. New improvements, including radios, siding, automobiles, running water, and electricity, were added to Amana homes, but the villages retained much of their communal-era atmosphere. In reorganizing the Society, the Amana people successfully reorganized their community, retaining what they felt were its best aspects while obliterating the distinctive features of communal ownership and labor that had characterized it for nearly a century.

In 1934, George C. Foerstner, the son of the High Amana storekeeper, began to sell and install refrigeration coolers from a small shed across the street from his father's store. By 1936, Foerstner and his single employee began to manufacture as well as to install these appliances under the name "Amana Electric Company," which was soon purchased by the Amana Society. Under Foerstner's continued management, and using Amana Society capital, the business grew to enormous proportions, marketing the first upright home freezer in 1947 and producing affordable home air-conditioning systems.

Photo circa 1970s by Joan Liffring-Zug Bourret

George C. Foerstner, president of Amana Refrigeration Inc., stands by America's first microwave oven, called the "Radarange," manufactured in Amana.

Sold by the Society in 1950, the company, headquartered in Middle Amana, grew to become the sixth-largest appliance manufacturer in the country, employing more than three thousand people. Two years after it merged with the Raytheon Corporation in 1965, Amana introduced the first home microwave oven.

A division of the Maytag Corporation since 2001, Amana Appliances remains a major presence in the Amana community. Additional workers came from outside the community, many relocating to the former communal garden and field sites surrounding the villages of Main and Middle Amana. The modern ranch-style homes that these individuals, as well as younger community residents, built in these new developments altered the Amana landscape.[38]

The Amana Society corporation has, itself, undergone many changes since 1932. Because of technological changes in farming, the seven communal-era districts have been combined under single management and now focus on commercial grain and livestock production. The seven original bakeries were consolidated into a single commercial bakery in Upper South Amana in 1942, and various other communal-era industries have long since been phased out. In 1971 the Society, in partnership with Nordstrom Oil Company, developed a complex of businesses near Interstate 80 called "Little Amana," a complex that includes a hotel, gas station, and shops.

Other changes came to the community in the years following the reorganization. During the 1930s, members of the Society organized Boy and Girl Scouts troops, and organizations such as the Homestead Welfare Club, the Amana Welfare Association, the Amana Community Club, and the Amana Young Men's Bureau provided diversions such as dances, picnics, and holiday programs. During World War II, the community forgot its pacifistic views and supported the war effort, sending more than 140 young men and women into military service, while Amana Refrigeration and the woolen mill filled government contracts.

Following the war, Amana became more and more like other small towns as residents bought television sets and two-tone automobiles, built new homes or remodeled former communal dwellings, and took summer vacations.

A further change came to the Amana community with the growth and development of tourism. The community had always been a popular destination for the curious, with more than 3,000 visitors a month touring the colonies during the last years of the communal era. Families from around the Midwest often spent entire weeks as guests in one of the Society's four hotels, and many lasting friendships formed between Amana residents and these visitors.

The number of outsiders coming to Amana increased with the development of improved roads in the 1920s. During the 1930s, the Amana Society built gas stations and sandwich shops to meet the needs of the traveling public. In 1934, a local entrepreneur converted the former Amana Hotel into the Colony Inn Restaurant, the first of what was to become a nationally famous series of Amana restaurants featuring "family-style dining." The Colony Inn was followed by the Ox Yoke Inn (1940), Zuber's Restaurant (1949), the Ronneburg Restaurant (1950), the Colony Marketplace (1968), the Brick Haus (1982), and finally, the Barn Restaurant in 1983.

The Colony Inn, the first of the famous restaurants that served family-style food like the kitchens of the communal era, opened in the early 1930s.

Amana women with husbands and boyfriends serving overseas pose in a "v" for victory formation during World War II.

Tourism boomed after World War II. Willie Dietrich plays the zither while the Oehler family, owners of the Ronneburg Restaurant, and staff sing in this 1970s photograph. Amana residents dressed in traditional German attire including the dirndl *to promote the tourist industry.*

By the 1960s, improved roadways, the addition of an interstate highway seven miles from the villages, the visibility given the name "Amana" due to its connection with the appliance company, and effective marketing brought hundreds of thousands of visitors to the villages each year. Local residents opened the first of several gift shops in 1960. An article in the December 1975 issue of the *National Geographic Magazine* as well as a positive 1981 story on the popular CBS "60 Minutes" broadcast were indicative of the wide publicity given to the community in those years.

In order to promote the community, local business leaders created a new organization, the Amana Colonies Travel Council (now the Amana Colonies Convention and Visitors' Bureau) in 1965 to print guide materials and oversee the marketing of the community. The new organization, together with local clubs, promoted the development of German-themed festivals such as Oktoberfest, first held in 1965, and Maifest.

Joan Liffring-Zug Bourret photo

Amana children perform at an early Oktoberfest, which was organized to develop tourism, in this 1970s photograph.

While these festivals were not a traditional part of life in Amana and represented customs against which Amana's forbearers rebelled, they did reflect the German customs that Amana residents became fascinated with as the century progressed. On a more historically accurate note, the Travel Bureau, together with the Iowa congressional delegation, successfully lobbied the Department of the Interior to designate the Amana Colonies a National Historic Landmark in 1965.

In part because of the new landmark status, as well as in response to growing commercialism, concerned Amana citizens of the 1960s tried to preserve the cultural fabric of the community. In 1968 a group formed the Amana Heritage Society, a nonprofit organization whose initial goal was to open a museum in the former Dr. Charles Noé residence in Main Amana. Since the museum opened in 1969, the Heritage Society has expanded its interpretative sites to include the Ruedy Communal Kitchen in Middle Amana in 1987, the Communal Agriculture Exhibit in South Amana in 1988, the Homestead Church in 1995, and the Homestead General Store in 2003. Additionally, the Heritage Society collects artifacts, original documents, and publications that have a bearing on the history of the community. In 1982, Heritage Society volunteers embarked on an ambitious oral history program during which they conducted interviews with more than 120 Amana residents about their memories of the communal period.

In 1977, the Amana Heritage Society hired a private consulting firm, Land and Community Associates, to develop a plan for the future preservation of the physical and structural remains of communal Amana. Concern for historic preservation led residents of six Amana villages to vote to create a special land-use district in 1983 to monitor development within the villages and to provide guidelines for future preservation, restoration, and commercial activity. An elected board oversees the land-use district and decides on requests for rezoning or the significant alteration or demolition of historic properties, as well as construction of new structures within the historic district. The Amana Historical Sites Foundation, created in 1994 as a nonprofit entity, owns several properties within the community and tries to find adaptive reuses for them.

Top: *Alma Ehrle is shown at her family winery, the first to open after the Great Change.* **Below:** *Workers at the Amana Meat Shop produce bratwurst from traditional recipes in a modern facility.*

The artistic heritage of the Amanas remains an important aspect of the community. The Amana Arts Guild, formed in 1978, has played an important role in preserving such traditional Amana folk arts as basketry, tin smithing, blacksmithing, carpet weaving, pottery, knitting, and quilt making, in addition to fine arts such as oil painting. Housed in the original High Amana meetinghouse, the Arts Guild sponsors art exhibits, classes, an annual arts festival, and an annual communal-style meal.

Craft Traditions Continue

Top: *The thrifty Amana people wove rugs with mill ends from the Woolen Mill as sisters Elsie Berger and Clara Mittelbach of South Amana are doing on a home loom. In 2001, Dorothy Trumpold, 89, an active rug weaver in East Amana, was honored by the National Endowment for the Arts with a National Heritage Fellowship.* ***Below:*** *South Amana neighbors Carrie Shoup, Clara Mittelbach, and Emma Setzer work on a traditional quilt.*

Joanna Schanz, above, revived the almost-lost art of Amana willow basketry in the Amana colonies. She leads workshops and is active in the Amana Arts Guild. The Schanz sandstone home is in the background. Two private furniture shops, together with the Amana Society Furniture Shop, continue the Amana tradition of hand-crafted furniture.

The publication of books on Amana photographers and a landmark study of Amana lithographer Joseph Prestele by art scholars outside the community have helped raise awareness of the community's rich artistic traditions. Artists from the world outside the community, including photographers Dorothea Lange and Joan Liffring-Zug Bourret, the painter Grant Wood, and others, have found an appealing subject in the Amanas.

Since the 1980s, many cultural and recreational outlets have helped expand the range of activities for both Amana residents and visitors. Beginning in 1988, the Old Creamery Theatre, a professional performing company founded at Garrison, Iowa, in 1971, has performed at the Price Creek Stage of the Amana Colonies Convention and Visitors' Bureau building. The Old Creamery provides an annual program of comedies and dramas, together with an acclaimed children's tour that reaches thousands of students in elementary schools across Iowa. In the summer of 2002 the Old Creamery opened a studio stage in the converted Amana depot for smaller productions.

The Old Creamery has been involved in presenting the history of the Amana community through many productions, including the successful *Old Colony Project,* in which costumed actors delivered monologues about communal life while serving guests a traditional Amana meal and, most notably, through the play *Home on the Iowa.* First produced in 2000, the play, which uses original letters, oral history recollections, and other accounts to describe communal life, was subsequently filmed and broadcast by Iowa Public Television.

Spearheaded by local residents, a nonprofit corporation, Amana Colonies Trails, has begun the process of developing recreational trails around the villages. The three-mile *Kolonieweg* trail, beginning at the Amana depot and winding around Lily Pond between Amana and Middle Amana, has been a popular feature of the community since it opened in 1998. Currently, residents are formulating plans for additional trails to connect the various villages.

A nature trail developed by the Amana Society winds through a timbered tract of land near Homestead. In addition to its natural features, the trail also highlights some of the extensive prehistoric remnants, including three earth mounds, left by early native inhabitants. A special feature of the nature trail is the scenic overlook of the Iowa River, which presents a view of the fish weir constructed by Native Americans some three hundred to four hundred years ago.

Funded, in part, by a grant from the state of Iowa, the Amana Main Street Project is a systematic program of street renovations whose goal is to return the streets of the village of Amana to an appearance more in keeping with the historic nature of the community. In 2002 the first phase of this project, the section of road connecting the woolen mill to the main village, was dedicated by residents and officials from local and state government. When completed, the streets will feature such historic features as wood board fences, lamps, and footbridges over ditches. Improved sanitary and utility features are also a part of the project.

Among its many projects, the Amana Heritage Society, in connection with the Amana Colonies Convention and Visitors' Bureau, produced a popular audio tour of the Amanas, highlighting sites of historic interest.

At the turn of the twentieth century, the Amana Society was touted as the largest and most successful communal society in the United States. With seven unadorned villages spread over a 26,000-acre domain, the Society managed to keep much of the world at bay while practicing its unique religious and social beliefs. A century later, however, the Amana Society still controlled a 26,000-acre domain, but its seven villages, now billed as "Iowa's most popular tourist attraction," were filled with gift shops and boutiques as well as the original buildings, homes, churches, and residents of the original community.

In the seventy years since its reorganization, the people of the Amana villages have acquired many of the standard accouterments of American life, including community clubs, Boy and Girl Scouts organizations, family vacations, automobiles, television, and other aspects of American consumer culture.

Today, the Amana Society is a diversified conglomeration of more than twenty local businesses, the majority of them predating the reorganization from communal life. In addition to a commercial bakery, the Society also maintains the Stone Hearth Bakery in Amana, the Amana Furniture Shop, the Amana Woolen Mill, the Amana General Store, the Homestead and Amana Meat Shops, the original communal-era farms (including the largest privately owned tract of forest land in Iowa), the local utility company, the Cedar Rapids Millwork Company, a restaurant, and other related businesses. Original Class A shareholders of the corporation continue to receive medical and burial benefits, although these benefits do not transfer with the shares once the original holder has died. The Amana Society is a publicly held corporation, and any interested party may purchase shares; ownership is not limited to Amana residents, descendants, or members of the Amana Church Society.

Joan Liffring-Zug Bourret photograph

Left: *Kitchen helpers are at a communal dinner reenactment, 1997, Amana Arts Guild.*

Below: *Emilie Hoppe, West Amana, photographed these Amana Church volunteers at the annual Christmas cookie walk, a church fund raiser.*

An Enduring Faith

Through all this change, the Amana Church has remained a potent force in the community. Although the majority of current church members are communal-era residents or their descendants, new converts join each year and the current membership exceeds four hundred, approximately a quarter of the current population of the villages.

In 1961, the church instituted an English-language service. Members today can attend services entirely in English or an early Sunday service that still features German hymns, prayers, and scripture reading. The introduction of an English-language service reflected the declining use of German among Amana's young people and the leadership's desire to meet the changing needs of the church community. Since the 1960s dedicated volunteers have spent countless hours translating the testimonies of the *Werkzeuge*, hymns, and other key religious writings of the Inspirationists.

Amana services still feature *a cappella* singing and are conducted by lay elders. Since 1987, both men and women have served as church elders. Although it is a voluntary gesture, many female churchgoers continue to wear the black cap, shoulder shawl, and apron traditionally worn by Amana women as a sign of humility, while men dress in dark business suits. Amana meetinghouse interiors retain the scrubbed pine floors, benches, and blue walls of communal times, while such additions as a fellowship space, modern office, and a sound system serve the changing needs of the church community.

Visitors are welcome at services, now held in Middle Amana for all seven villages. The Main Amana meetinghouse is used by the church for special combined services, weddings, funerals, and as a Sunday school. At death, members of the Amana Church Society are still buried in chronological order of death in their respective village cemeteries, which do not feature family plots. Graves are still marked with plain concrete markers giving name, date of death, and age, while hedges of pine trees still surround these quiet resting places.

Joan Liffring-Zug Bourret photograph

Wilhelmine Dickel Setzer (1888–1982) lived adjacent to and took care of the High Amana meetinghouse until her death. The striped wool carpet on the plain wooden floor is woven in the traditional style of the Amana weavers. House plants in the window belonged to Mrs. Setzer. The meetinghouse now houses the Amana Arts Guild.

Endnotes

[1] Gottlieb Scheuner, *Inspirations Historie, 1817–1850*. Trans. by Janet W. Zuber (Amana, Iowa: Amana Church Society, 1987), 3.

[2] Scheuner, *Inspirations Historie, 1817–1850*. 5, 12.

[3] Scheuner, *Inspirations Historie, 1817–1850*, 23–24, 38. The standard biography of Metz is Francis Alan DuVal, "Christian Metz: German-American Religious Leader and Pioneer."(Ph.D. diss., State University of Iowa, 1948.)

[4] Scheuner, *Inspirations Historie, 1817–1850*, 42, 48, 53–54.

[5] Jonathan Andelson, "Communalism and Change in the Amana Society, 1855–1932" (Ph.D diss., University of Michigan, 1974), 38; Scheuner, *Inspirations Historie, 1817–1850*, 59.

[6] Scheuner, *Inspirations Historie, 1817–1850*, 72, 81; Barthinius L Wick, "Christian Communism in the Mississippi Valley: The Amana Society, or Community of True Inspiration," *Midland Monthly* 6 (October 1896), 338.

[7] Wilhelm Noé to "Brothers and Fellow Members," 22 December 1842, trans. Peter Stuck, collection of the author.

[8] Charles F. Noé, "A Brief History of the Amana Society," *Iowa Journal of History and Politics* 2 (April 1904): 176; DuVal, "Christian Metz," 119.

[9] Scheuner, *Inspirations Historie*, 221; Joseph Prestele to Martin Prestele, 15 October 1843, translation by Magdalena Oehl Schuerer, Translation Collection, Amana Heritage Society.

[10] H. A. P., "German Ebenezer Society," *The Cultivator*, 8 August 1847, 248.

[11] Andelson, "Communalism and Change," 57; Christian Metz to Mr. Fabricus, 5 November 1855, trans. Magdalena Schuerer, Translation Collection, Amana Heritage Society.

[12] For the Hydraulic Association controversy see Hoehnle, Peter, "A Machine in the Garden: The Woolen Textile Industry of the Amana Society, 1785–1942," *Annals of Iowa* 61 (Winter 2002): 24–67.

[13] Christian Metz to Mr. Fabricus, 5 November 1855.

[14] Millard Fillmore to General G. B. Sergeant, 1 December 1854, Millard Fillmore papers, volume 2.

[15] Andelson, "Communalism and Change," 73–74.

[16] DuVal, "Christian Metz," 252.

[17] Oral History #18, typed transcript, Oral History Collection, Amana Heritage Society.

[18] Oral History #2, typed transcript, Oral History Collection, Amana Heritage Society.

[19] Oral History #8, typed transcript, Oral History Collection, Amana Heritage Society.

[20] Henry A. Wallace, "Visiting the Amana Society," *Wallaces' Farmer*, 18 December 1914, 1652.

[21] Henry A. Wallace, "Visiting the Amana Society," *Wallaces' Farmer*, 1 January 1915, 9.

[22] Oral History #50, typed transcript, Oral History Collection, Amana Heritage Society.

[23] Henry A. Wallace, "Visiting the Amana Society," *Wallaces' Farmer*, 18 December 1914, 1652; Jonathan Andelson, "From the Wetterau to Ebenezer and Amana: A Demographic Profile of the Inspirationists in America." In *Emigration and Settlement Patterns of German Communities in North America*." Ed. by Eberhard Reichmann, LaVern Rippley, and Jorg Nagler. (Indianapolis: Indiana University, 1995), 68.

[24] Quoted in Richard, Lord Acton and Patricia Nassif Acton, *To Go Free: A Treasury of Iowa's Legal Heritage* (Ames: Iowa State University Press, 1995), 200.

[25] *Marengo Sentinel*, 26 February and 5 March 1918.

[26] Oral History, #25 and #34, typed transcripts, Oral History Collection, Amana Heritage Society.

[27] *Des Moines Register*, 22 October 1933.

[28] William F. Moershel, "Statement of Liquitable Assets and Liabilities," 4 April 1931, author's collection.

[29] Oral History #33; Oral History #31, typed transcripts, Oral History Collection, Amana Heritage Society.

[30] Minutes, Amana Society Board of Trustees, 16 March 1931, Amana Society Archives, Amana Society main office, Main Amana. Lawrence Rettig, *Amana Today: A History of the Amana Society from 1932 to the Present* (Amana: Amana Society, 1975), 123.

[31] *Reorganization Plan* (Middle Amana, Iowa: Amana Society, 1932.)

[32] Emilie Zuber Hoppe, "A Story Recalled," unpublished paper, Amana Heritage Society, 1981, 13. Oral History #20.

[33] Bertha M. H. Shambaugh, "Amana–In Transition," *Palimpsest* 17 (May 1936): 184.

[34] Iowa County Land Deed Records, Book 81/82, pp. 213–23, Iowa County Recorder's Office, Marengo, Iowa. Oral History #57.

[35] *Amana Society Bulletin*, 2 June 1932. Oral Histories #6 and #20, typed transcripts, Oral History Collection, Amana Heritage Society.

[36] Shambaugh, "Amana–In Transition," 155; *Amana Society Bulletin*, 14 July and 1 September 1932; Oral History #57, typed transcript, Oral History Collection, Amana Heritage Society.

[37] Shambaugh, "Amana–In Transition," 151; Oral History #59, typed transcript, Oral History Collection, Amana Heritage Society.

[38] Rettig, *Amana Today*, 43–47. Clifford Trumpold. "65 Years at Amana Refrigeration: Building the American Dream," *Willkommen* 16 (Late Summer, 1997): 8–9.

A Select Bibliography

The sources included in this essay, with a few exceptions, are all in print and, together with several other fine books, are available through the Amana Heritage Society, Amana, Iowa.

The interested reader is encouraged to explore the many scholarly and other articles written about Amana, particularly those found in the excellent publication of the Communal Studies Association, *Communal Societies*.

General Works on Communal Societies

Hinds, William Alfred. *American Communities*. New York: Corinth Books, 1961. (Reprint of 1878 edition.)

Nordhoff, Charles. *The Communistic Societies of the United States: From Personal Observations*. New York: Dover, 1966. (Reprint of 1875 edition.)

America's Communal Utopias. Edited by Donald E. Pitzer Chapel Hill: The University of North Carolina Press, 1997.

Published Works about Amana

Andelson, Jonathan G. "The Gift To Be Single: Celibacy and Religious Enthusiasm in the Community of True Inspiration," *Communal Societies* 5 (1985): 1–32.

Bourret, Joan Liffring-Zug. *The Amanas: A Photographic Journey, 1959–1999*. Iowa City: Penfield Press, 1999.

——ed. *Life In Amana: Reporters' Views of the Communal Way, 1867–1935*. Iowa City, Iowa: Penfield Press, 1998.

Garrett, Clarke. *Origins of the Shakers: From the Old World to the New World* Baltimore: Johns Hopkins Press, 1987.

Grossmann, Walter. "The Origins of the True Inspired of Amana." *Communal Societies* 4 (1984)*: 133–149*.

Hoehnle, Peter A. "A Machine in the Garden: The Woolen Textile Industry of the Amana Society, 1785–1942." *Annals of Iowa* 61 (Winter 2002): 24–67.

——"Carl Flick and Grant Wood: A Regionalist Friendship in Amana." *Iowa Heritage Illustrated* 82 (Spring 2001), 2–19.

——"Community in Transition: Amana's Great Change, 1931–1933." *Annals of Iowa* 60 (Winter 2001): 1–34.

Hoppe, Emilie. *Seasons of Plenty: Amana Communal Cooking*. Ames: Iowa State University Press, 1994.

Lankes, Frank J. *The Ebenezer Community of True Inspiration*. Buffalo, New York: Kiesling Publishing Company, 1949.

Liffring-Zug, Joan. *The Amanas Yesterday: A Religious Communal Society*. Iowa City: Penfield Press, 1975. Reprint, Iowa City: Penfield Books, 2003.

Ohrn, Steven. *Remaining Faithful: Amana Folk Art in Transition*. Des Moines: Iowa Department of Cultural Affairs, 1988.

Perkins, William Rufus and Barthinius Wick. *History of the Amana Society or Community of True Inspiration*. Iowa City: State University of Iowa, 1891.

Rettig, Lawrence L. *Amana Today: A History of the Amana Colonies from 1932 to Present*. Amana, Iowa: Amana Society, 1975.

Scheuner, Gottlieb. *Inspirations Historie, vol. 1714–1728*. Translated by Janet W. Zuber. Amana: Amana Church Society, 1977.

——*Inspirations Historie, vol. II, 1729–1817*. Translated by Janet W. Zuber. Amana: Amana Church Society, 1978.

——*Inspirations Historie, vol. III, 1817–1850*. Translated by Janet W. Zuber. Amana: Amana Church Society, 1987.

——*Barbara Heinemann Landmann Biography and E. L. Gruber's Teachings on Divine Inspiration and Other Essays*. Translated by Janet W. Zuber. Amana: Amana Church Society, 1981.

Shambaugh, Bertha M. H. *Amana: The Community of True Inspiration*. Iowa City, Iowa: State Historical Society of Iowa, 1908. (Reprint, Iowa City: State Historical Society of Iowa, 1988)

Webber, Philip E. *Kolonie-Deutsch: Life and Language in Amana*. Ames: Iowa State University Press, 1993.

Yambura, Barbara Selzer and Eunice W. Bodine. *A Change and a Parting: My Story of Amana*. Ames: Iowa State University Press, 1960. Reprint, Iowa City: Penfield Press, 2001.

Unpublished Works

Andelson, Jonathan G. "Communalism and Change in the Amana Society, 1855–1932." Ph.D. dissertation, University of Michigan, 1974.

DuVal, Francis Alan. "Christian Metz: German-American Religious Leader and Pioneer." Ph.D. dissertation, University of Iowa, 1948.

Moore, Frank M. "The Amana Society: Accommodation of Old World Beliefs in a New World Frontier Setting." Ph.D. dissertation. Nashville: Vanderbilt University, 1988.

Schnieder, Ulf-Michael. "Die wahren 'Propheten-Kinder" Sprache, Literatur und Wirkung der Inspirierten im 18. Jahrhundert." Ph.D. dissertation, University of Goettingen, Germany, 1992.

West Amana Store   *Amana Woolen Mill*

What survives of the old Amana today are the memories of its communal survivors, of which there are fewer each year; the physical environment that those communal workers created; and the enduring visions of faith, work, and hope expressed by its founders.

Wer Jesum Bei Sich Hat

Artist Joseph Prestele created this image of the ship *Florida*, on which his family, and hundreds of other Inspirationists, came to the United States in the 1840s. During one bitter passage, a group of Inspirationists sang this hymn, by Christian Connow, which remains an enduring song of religious feeling in the Amana Church today:

If Jesus walks with you
What does it matter
How dark the day may be
Or bad the weather?
If Jesus walks with you
You're filled with gladness
For comfort fills the heart
And bans all sadness

If Jesus walks with you
You're bound for heaven
No greater wealth this world
Has ever given
Your happiness will show
Through tears and sorrow
If you anticipate
That great tomorrow.

Translation: Wilhelmine Baumgartner

Collection of the Amana Heritage Society.

Joseph Prestele, Sr., 1850: Detail from "The Wanderings of the Inspirationists,"
lithograph drawn on stone

96—